Walk In Your NOW

Aundrae T. Shaw

Copyright © 2012 Aundrae T. Shaw

All rights reserved.

ISBN: **0615964176**
ISBN-13: **978-0615964171**

DEDICATION

This book is dedicated to my son, Aundrae T. Shaw Jr, "AJ", who has always totally believed in me to fulfill my God given purpose. I am thankful for your unwavering love and support, even though we truly did not understand fully what God has in store for our lives.

During the times when it seemed like we would never reach the next level fulfilling the dreams and purpose God gave me to fulfill. You are the one thing that drives me to become everything God has intended for me to become in the earth for you, my son. Your love is encouragement, and I want you to become all God has in store for you to become as well. God will keep our sons until Jesus comes.

Without your belief and complete trust in what God has said to me, He would do for us, drives me into seeking God religiously. Even more, the love of Jesus keeps me seeking Him daily; to please God I live.

AJ, I love you and I am grateful to have such a great loving son and friend. God will keep His word! Believe in Him, you know His voice.

Walk in your NOW

"Foundational Principles to Kingdom LIVING on Earth"

Intro to

Developing a Kingdom Mindset to Govern the Earth for God

"The Son has Called for the Sons to Stand"

The interdiction book to Governing with a Kingdom Mindset

"WALKING IN YOU NOW"

When your heart believes, you need to have the right thought-life to live life to the full. Jesus did so that we can learn how to walk on the earth under the Government of your King Yahweh. There is no limit to where the truth will take you having: understanding, wisdom, knowledge. To have stewardship over Kingdom: wealth, strength, power. Living on the earth the way Jesus desires you to live, were you have growth both physically and spiritually, having lasting success, living in complete freedom on earth.

Walk in your NOW

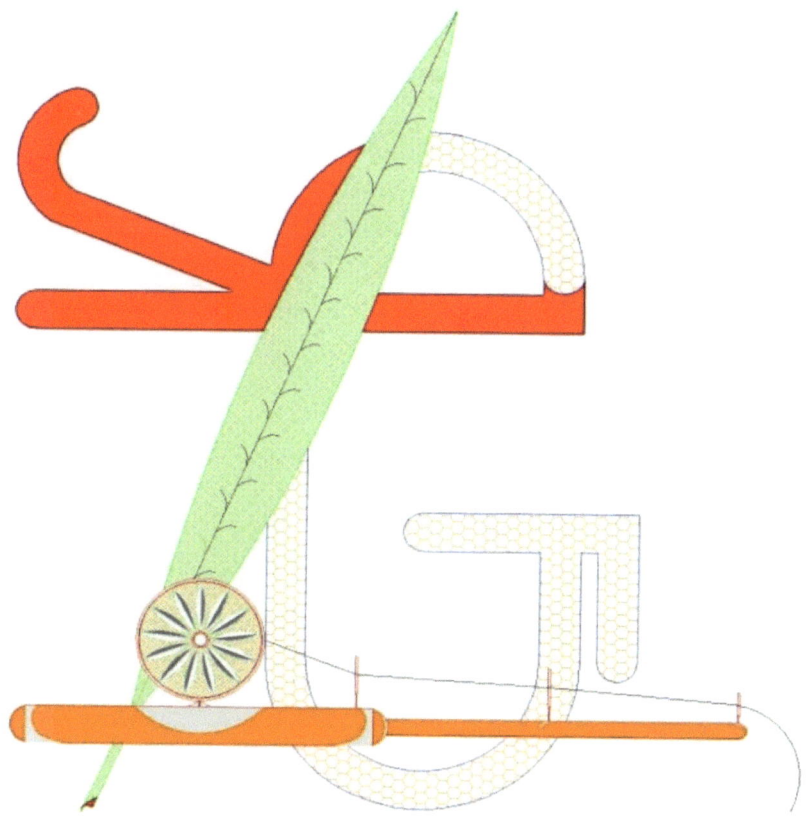

CONTENTS

	Acknowledgments	i
1	The Intent for this Book	10
2	Knowing your Saved	26
3	What is Faith	33
4	Applying your Faith	41
5	Now Faith	47
6	Walk in Your **NOW**	53
7	The Plan that Works	59
8	What God Wants	63
9	Unforgiveness	70
10	The Investment	76
11	About the Author	101

ACKNOWLEDGMENTS

I would like to take this time and give thanks to my Father, Yahweh. The one true God who has made Heaven and Earth; I praise you Jesus, for dying for the sins of the whole world. To the Holy Spirit, well, what could I be without you in my life and leading me daily?

I thank you for reading these words of life. I do pray these words will renew your heart, reviving your mind to govern with a Kingdom Mindset from NOW on.

Let's Get Real Ministry believes in Building Houses of Refuge, where hurting people can come to a place to physically feel the LOVE of Jesus through other people who are filled with Jesus' love.

Read these words until you have received all that the Holy Spirit has placed here for you to gain. Then, follow the leading of the Holy Spirit to bless someone else.

I ask the Holy Spirit, "To put this book in the hands of Kings and Queens, and in the hands of people who will believe and live a lifestyle of faith to enable the Kingdom of Jesus to grow with strong, faith filled believers. It is time to prepare for the arrival of our King Jesus' return. I pray of the whole body to walk in their NOW with understanding, as one body, having one likeness, fulfilling one motive, having one Mindset to please the heart of God."

> *"₅ But the Lord came down to see the city and the tower which the sons of men had built. 6 And the Lord said, "Indeed the people are one and they all have one language, and this is what they begin to do; now nothing that they propose to do will be withheld from them." Genesis 11:5, 6 KJV*

My dream is, this time we the children of God will have the heart of God; walking in the love of Jesus, wanting to live life for the Father on earth allowing Jesus to be our King, allowing the will of the Father, having Heaven on Earth.

The Kingdom must go forth!

Know and believe all things must bow a knee to the name of Jesus.

Amen

THE INTENT FOR THIS BOOK

I would like to thank you for taking time from your busy life to read these words of encouragement. I pray that these words will give you hope and empowerment to press on to your higher calling in God's Kingdom.

The intent is not just for another religious teaching, pushing you into a religious methodology, or denomination, or keeping deviation in the body of Christ.

The intent is for you to have a relationship with Jesus the Christ. Worshiping One God, in One Spirit, having One Mindset!

I pray you really interpret what you are about to read. This will change your life forever! There's only ONE God, with the keys to eternal life in Heaven. Heaven and Hell both are very real places! His son, Jesus holds the keys to life, to obtain everlasting life in the new earth. Jesus Is God's Word made into Flesh. Yes Jesus is God's only begotten son. He was born by a virgin and walked on the earth. He was baptized, killed and was resurrected from the dead by the power of God. He NOW sets on the right hand of God the Father forever more. I pray you will keep reading this book it is not just another religious book. Yes, there are many ways to do one thing on earth. Life on earth is about a having a real RELATIONSHIP with Jesus, the Christ, not about going to church, becoming religious.

When I truly meet Jesus, I want to become a shining light in a world full of darkness for Him. I want to become the best candle that God Himself has set on a candle stick to shine in the world, drawing all men unto Christ with love. I want to fulfill my purpose by empowering all of God's children to go and carry the good news of Jesus Kingdom, where all will see life lived before them holy because of obedience to God's love. I pray everyone who does not know Christ will want to follow Christ because of what they will see from my life on earth. I pray to help in leading all that will believe in Jesus to a house of rescue.

I pray whoever does not know Christ can find refuge from a world full of pain in Christ Jesus. Coming into a relationship filled with Christ's love, where one can feel the love of Christ through a believing body physically. I will equip everyone and everything God allows to cross my path with His word, to stand with power, knowing how to use the power within to change any and every circumstance in life, by speaking the Word of God out their mouth to every circumstance in faith, having a real relationship with God, having confidence in God's power where they will see physical manifestation of their faith in God come to pass in their life time.

To have confidence in the words spoken from their mouth, knowing their eyes will see their words become physical in earth, because they have spoken the will of God for their life. I want every person I meet to know and love Jesus. I want you to know how to use your mouth to speak the Word of God in faith, seeing practical application of biblical principles.

I want every person I meet to become a disciple for Christ Jesus, knowing they are set: over nations, over kingdoms, to root out, to pull down, to destroy, to throw down, to build up, and plant seeds of faith in everything that cross their paths as well. I just want every person to know, and believe that Jesus loves them, and He died for them making them free from any sin.

Hear me, and hear me good my brothers and sisters, when Jesus comes back, He is not coming back friendly! He is coming to destroy everything that is not in, or like Him, then to make a Heaven and NEW EARTH!

You must have a real relationship with Jesus. God named Jesus my Christ, as the true Lord, Our only King and only Savior! Once you read through these words you'll see only one thing! GOD! MY Daddy does not put anything in your hands, you must work for it. He blesses what your hands are doing. He gives you the opportunity to believe, so you will then do. I want to see the power of God working through you were what you said happen! Because of your belief in Jesus you have obtains power so walk in your NOW. Because of Who, and What, My Creator has said you are to Him power is available to you when you believe!

I want to see every broken heart fixed not patch! My Farther is very faithful to any one that will believe. God gave me the plans and instructions for "Lets Get Real" by asking me the question. He said, "Do you remember what you told me when you were five?" I said, "Yes." Then, He told me to be real before His people, by showing His people His love, helping all to obtain a Kingdom Mindset. He told me that He allowed me to become a builder to

Walk in your NOW

understand the hard work construction takes.

Now, I am to empower people to believe in the power of God working within them. Through your belief you will change your own life from inside out, you will become an infection to everyone around changing their lives because of your belief in the power within. He the voice spoke things that I am writing down even as you are reading this book.

God's Spirit has chosen me to empower His people to believe, and to build immaculate temples that His people can enjoy worshipping Him in and to maintain the building. He said, "Son if you love Me, renew the minds of my children with my Living Word. I will make your name great among men."

He told me to teach: Faith, Power, and Love. He said, "Teach my lambs to lead my sheep's back until me." He told me to make disciples after God's own heart, to love Him, and want to obey his every word. He said, "Son, teach my children to live holy lives before Me." He said, "Son, I want my whole body to worship Me in Spirit, and Truth, with complete Unity as one body having no longer many belief, but having a real relationship with Me as their God." He said, "I want the world to see the power of unity once more; I want my body to walk, talk, even the more to live unified."

He said son, "Tell them it is time for my body to become ONE in Me, where He can be in them, and they in He." He told me to tell every nation in the world, teaching the power of Unity until, He come for His children. Jesus will take all of His children that have believed in Him, into His secret place until He has fulfilled every part of His Word in the earth.

God told me to be real before His people. He told me, my life has become the ministry. He has entrusted me to oversee on the earth. I grew up in a Baptist church and I heard ministers talk about Jesus, but didn't live like Jesus. They talked about how powerful God is, but never experienced the true power of God where: blind eyes were opened, or lame legs walked, even where any type of sickness dried up, because the man of God spoke it to be so.

Being what God has allowed me to know about Him, even to see, I promised God, I would become a living sacrifice for Him in the earth so all will see the power of believing and obeying the Word of God to be the only truth on the earth. To show believers, even unbelievers the same, the real power that lives in anyone who believes in Jesus.

If they confessed Jesus as their Lord and choose to live a life of obedience before God on the earth, then they will be given all power. How can God deny Himself? I promised to teach others to become a living, obedient vessel, willing to be used by God, obeying His every command, doing what He has told them to do, the way He has told them to do it, to see real power in the earth because of obedience.

God will then bless His faithful sons, adding unto them what is needed to accomplish the purposes He has made them to do on the earth. God has shown me in His word, and He has told me that this ministry will show people how to truly be led by the Holy Spirit. We will see physically the power of God as in the old, where we can pray and physical fire will come from heaven. So sons of God, it is time to stand, and use the power God has given, to walk in your now.

The earth awaits the sons of God to walk as Jesus walked. The earth awaits true believers to stand on their faith and live before God holy. The earth is waiting on unity in the Body of Christ. God is calling unto you to become so Jesus gets the glory of your life Now.

This book is to ignite your faith in pushing you or to strengthen your belief in your relationship with your Heavenly Father God. I pray you grow, strengthening your confidence in the power that lives inside of you. I pray these words will strengthen will every area needing strength, given the Holy Spirit seeds to give life to.

This book will help you in one of two things: developing a real relationship with Jesus and to know the power of God that lives on the inside of you. Will you choose to NOW live for your Heavenly Father on earth? I desire for you to speak with Him daily, seeking His divine guidance.

These words will become mighty seeds, being planted in your heart, which will grow into mighty trees, producing fruitful thoughts for the Kingdom of God to move with power!

Upon completion of reading these words, your Mindset will change, developing your mind into a Kingdom Mindset, where the Word of God renews your thought process to become one with how Jesus thought when He walked on the earth.

Hopefully you know what God has spoken to you. Your purpose is on the earth as a part of the Body of Christ, becoming more effective in the fields God has called you to each day, as the Holy Spirit leads you to harvest the fields, teaching you all of the spiritual truths in Jesus.

I know your heart will become receptive to the simplicity of the concepts and principals of God's spoken words NOW. God's spoken word is the only truth that should govern our every thought. God's written word will change your life forever, enhancing your perception of your circumstances. You will see your life how God thought your life should be before He spoke His first words, creating the Heavens and Earth.

I have asked my Heavenly Father to put these words in this book, into your hands NOW, so you can desire to have a Kingdom Mindset, which will drive you to become faithful to the things of God. You want to become One with Christ, to see God's Glory, Power, and Majesty fill the earth; His children have become One in Mind, Body, and Spirit. We are showing Him we are faithful to His will for our lives, so then God's plans for heaven to be in the earth will truly exist!

I've asked my Father to put these words of love into your hands, for you to know, "It Is Your Time, Walk In Your NOW!"

THE INSPIRATION

These words were inspired by the Holy Spirit to be written in this book after I attended a spirit lead revival at Christ Temple International in Lawrenceville, Georgia. Even though CTI was an assignment to me by God; I received a word from God to empower the body of Christ as a whole, developing dedicated solders for the Kingdom of Jesus Christ to plant words of life to strengthen my fellow brothers and sisters in our faith walk here on earth; having the Living Word of God, working on our behalf in our daily lives.

God has asked me to become His Gospel, applying His word to my life allowing my life to show and teach others without me saying a word. He showed me the importance of Living, and speaking His word; He showed me how important it is to be led by His Holy Spirit, being led by His Spirit is the only way to live a Holy life on the earth. He said, "I must become a living sacrifice, to empower every believer and unbeliever the same to receive a desire to become a living sacrifice unto God which is our reasonable service,"

> *"1. So here's what I want you to do, God helping you: Take your everyday ordinary life-your sleeping, eating, going to work, and walking around life-and place it before God as an offering. Embracing what God does for you is the best thing you can do for him 2. Don't become so well-adjusted to your culture that you fit into it without even thinking. Instead, fix your attention on God. You'll be changed from the inside out. Readily recognize what he wants from you, and quickly respond to it. Unlike the culture around you, always dragging you down to its level of immaturity, God brings the best out of you, develops well-former maturity in you."* Romans 12:1, 2 MSG

Learning to enjoy a life driven by obedience to the Living Word of God will become you, allowing the Holy Spirit to guide your every thought; this is my only desire my friend. The beginning of having a life filled with lasting substance starts with you choosing to be obedient to the Holy Spirit of God. Living a life wanting nothing having every need met, walking in true abundance enjoying the life Jesus, gave those who believe in him; by hanging on a tree for every believer to truly liberated in Him.

Allowing every thought to become subdued by the living Word of God, so the Spirit of God can give life to the Word of God living with-in your belly NOW, allowing your everyday life's chooses to give glory to the Son of God, Jesus the Christ becoming more like Him daily.

These words of faith sown, NOW includes teaching and developing your thought life to become one with Christ; developing a Kingdom Mindset is, teaching your thoughts to line up with the Living Words of God, speaking what you believe with instance corresponding actions. Your new mindset will NOW give the Holy Spirit of God divine words to give life to, framing your worlds around you.

Once you have believed in the Living Word of God working on your behalf; know the Holy Spirit gives life to the will or word of God spoken out of your mouth. You showing intense corresponding actions to your faith in the well of your Heavenly Father have spoken to you. Then you will see God put His super on top of your natural, to see Gods' will manifest before your very eyes physically in the earth NOW. Becoming one with the

Walk in your NOW

Living Word of God becomes your only desire, once you have falling in love with Jesus.

You will live to achieve God's will for your life in the earth until Jesus returns, or you go to sleep. Living with a Kingdom Mindset is living how God desire you to live, with revelation of His Living Word being spoken, with action seeing God Word working in your life daily. Believing and knowing who and what Jesus did, this is the key to having eternal life. Applying the Word of God to your everyday living, with action is required to see your faith become physical. God knew you even before your mom and dad thought of bring you into this world.

> "4. *This is what God said:* 5. **Before I shaped you in the womb, I knew all about you. Before you saw the light of day, I had holy plans for you: A prophet to the nations - that's what I had in mind for you.**" *Jeremiah 1: 4-5 MSG*

Choosing to apply basic application of the Word of God with love, changes your every daily thoughts to line up with God's Living Word, so your actions must follow. What is a Kingdom Mindset, simply put to having the mind of Christ Jesus, allowing the Living Word of God to govern your every thought, knowing that the Holy Spirit will judges every thought, because your thought make actions.

> *"15. But he that is spiritual judgeth all things, yet he himself is judged of no man. 16. For who hath known the mind of the Lord, that he may instruct him? But we have the mind of Christ." 1 Corinthians 2:15, 16 KJV*

A Kingdom Mindset starts when you know everything you NOW see, God thought them before He spoke them into existence. Knowing and believing what you say will manifest before you physically good or bad is the begging of Kingdom Living. Because God thought it, then He spoke it out loud, NOW we see it before our eyes today physically. That is the same power that lives in you as a child of the Living God.

> *"3. By Faith, we see the world called into existence by God's word, what we see created by*

Walk in your NOW

what we don't see." Hebrews 11:3 MSG

These words are seedling seeds, which the Spirit of God will use to change your life forever, once you have believed. The Spirit of God will give life to these words so your faith, will manifest before your eyes physically.

The Spirit of God will give life to the Word of God through you speaking the word of God in faith. The Holy Spirit will give the Living Word of God spoken out of your mouth life; if you believe in the Living Word of God feeding your hope, you speaking the Living Word of God with your mouth in faith, the Holy Spirit will give your words substance to appear before you to frame the worlds around you.

Once you believe in speaking the Living Word of God, Gods' Spirit gives life to the words you speak; the Holy Spirit needs the instruction, and your agreement of The Living Word of God being spoken out your moth to have lasing result, showing the power of words being spoken. Without The Living Word of God He, the Holy Spirit cannot create substance, and without the Holy Spirit the Living Word cannot literally appear before you physically.

> *"21. Death and life are in the power of the tongue: and they that love it shall eat the fruit thereof." Proverbs 18:21 KJV*

The Holy Spirit can only give life to The Living Word of God that lives within your heart; without God's Word living within your heart, God's Spirit cannot frame the will of God for your life in the earth.

Your words without the Living Word of God living within you are: powerless, void, useless and empty. If you are not speaking the Living Word of God, it is not God's Spirit given life to what you NOW see. Remember what you say will appear before you, good or bad. The Holy Spirit only gives life to the Living Word of God being spoken out of your mouth.

> *7. And the LORD God formed man of the dust of the ground, and breathed into his nostrils the breath of life; and man became a living soul. Genesis 2:7 KJV*

It is the Holy Spirit who gives life to the faith filled

words you are speaking from Gods' will for your life, it is the Spirit of God, that has framed what you physically see before your eyes NOW; this is why you must: learn of, believe in, and allowing the Living Word of God to live in you as the only TRUTH, you should make every decision from the Living Word of God. You are made in the image of God, having the co-creating power of God within you. I'm trying to ignite that power that lives inside of every believer, so the Kingdom can move with power. Gods Kingdom is not just words spoken with no action being seen from the words we speak.

We must know what to speak so the Holy Spirit can give life to then see the lasting results of spoken words. You are a co-creator of the world's physically framed on the earth by the words you will speak lead by the Holy Spirit.

"4. These are the generations of the heavens and of the earth when they were created, in the day that the LORD God made the earth and the heavens," Genesis 2:4 KJV

> "*5. Thus saith God the LORD, he that created the heavens, and stretched them out; he that spread forth the earth, and that which cometh out of it; he that giveth breath unto the people upon it, and spirit to them that walk therein:" Isaiah 42:5 KJV*

> "*18. For thus saith the LORD that created the heavens; God himself that formed the earth and made it; he hath established it, he created it not in vain, he formed it to be inhabited: I am the LORD; and there is none else." Isaiah 45:18 KJV*

What you are seeing from the words you have been speaking have appear before you good or bad; once you become obedient to the Holy Spirit you will then access the creating power that is within you. Believing in the Living Word of God being spoken by you, makes the difference.

The amount of God's Living Word you have believed in your heart, gives you hope to speak God's word out loud in faith to see the Holy Spirit give life to the faith filled words you will speak.

Walk in your NOW

The Holy Spirit is the life giver; to the words you will speak in faith from Gods' Word; the Holy Spirit gives faith filled words life to become physical, so they will appearing before your eyes physically NOW.

> "63. *It is the Spirit Who gives life [He is the Life-giver]; The words (truths) that I have been speaking to you are spirit and life.*"
> St. John 6:63 AMP

NO, God's Spirit has not, and will not, give life to words spoken out of an unstable emotional state of mind. God's Spirit will only give life to words spoken with in His will; His Holy Spirit has inspired men to write about Him and His well for our lives to know God and to know His will for our lives.

He written word is so we can learn of Him having examples of how He has worked on man behalf in the past. His written Word is Gods' plans and purposes for all of His children's lives on earth. The spirit of the world is responsible for the things appearing before you outside of God's will for your life.

The adversary gives life to all the evil and bad things

we NO. The same way you have the power to co-create God's will for your life the adversary uses your mouth to frame all the pain, and evil to get you not to believe in your Heavenly Farther plans and will for your life.

> "*10. A thief is only there to steal and kill and destroy. I came so they can have real and eternal life, more and better life than they ever dreamed of. 11. I am the Good Shepherd puts the sheep before himself, sacrifices himself if necessary. John 10:10, 11 MSG*

The thief cannot allow you to understand the true power of speaking God's word in faith, having intense corresponding action to line up with what you have believed. He knows what you NOW see, comes from what you have been speaking.

His whole plan is to; test you to the limit to get you not to trust in Gods' Living Word not being true. He plan is to see if you will curse God to His face because of your NOW circumstances'. He wants you to speak foolishly, He don't want you to speak God's word: trusting in God, or to believing in God's Word working on your behalf in the earth.

He wants you to have intense corresponding action to follow you fear, and unbelieveth. He cannot allow you to believe in the Living Word of God working on your behalf.

> *"11. But put forth thine hand now, and touch all that he hath, and he will curse thee to thy face." Job 1:11 KJV*

Remember what you are speaking good or bad will appear before you, I pray you NOW only speak the Words the Holy Spirit give you to speak, God's Spirit is the giver of life not death. You should allow the Living Word of God to govern, or to control your every thought. Your thought will then only produce life and the words you speak will frame the worlds around you, being led by the Holy Spirit.

> *"8. For he who sows to his own flesh (lower nature, sensuality) will from the flesh reap decay and ruin and destruction, but he who sows to the Spirit*

will from the Spirit reap eternal life. 9. And let us not lose heart and grow weary and faint in acting nobly and doing right, for in due time and at the appointed season we shall reap, if we do not loosen and relax our courage and faint. 10. So then, as occasion and opportunity open up to us, let us do good [morally] to all people [not only being useful or profitable to them, but also doing what is for their spiritual good and advantage]. Be mindful to be a blessing, especially to those of the household of faith [those who belong to God's family with you, the believers]."
Galatians 6:8-10 AMP

I know that these words of Faith are renewing your mind and developing your mind to become one with Christ's. So then your thoughts, even more the words you are speaking will become a lethal weapon for the Kingdom of God. Your words will be used to destroy every seed the devil has influence you to speak.

Changing everything that is around you NOW; NOW every word you speak will give glorify the Son of God Jesus our Christ, by renewing the words you will NOW think to say.

Walk in your NOW

Changing what you speak out of your mouth from NOW on. I know you will surrender to the Holy Spirit to guide you in your thought process by the Word of God; so your thoughts will line up with the Living Word of God in your everyday actions NOW.

Because you have received life from the Living Word of God being spoken from your mouth, framing worlds around you NOW, framing your world to line up with God's plans for your life.

The Spirit of God gives life to faith filled words that are spoken out of your mouth in faith, the words cannot be seen until spoken, allowing the Spirit of God to give them life so they can change the things that are seen for the glory of Jesus' life on earth.

The Spirit will give life to the Living Word of God, the Holy Spirit will give substance to your faith, your faith must have intense corresponding action on your behalf to show your believeth in Gods' Living Word working on your behalf.

These seedling seeds will empower you to speak the Word of God, speaking the only truth that will last for all eternity. God has given you the authority to change the worlds you see because He has made you in His image.

> *"27. So God created man in his own image, in the image of God created he him; male and female created he them. 28. And God blessed them, and God said unto them, Be fruitful, and multiply, and replenish the earth, and subdue it: and have dominion over the fish of the sea, and over the fowl of the air, and over every living thing that moveth upon the earth." Genesis 1:27, 28 KJV*

From today on speak faith filled words, knowing and believing the Spirit of God will give those words life enabling your words to frame worlds you see NOW to glorify the Living God Jesus.

> *"5. Let this same attitude and purpose and [humble] mind be in you which was in Christ Jesus: [Let Him be your example in humility:] 6. Who, although being essentially one with God and in the form of God [possessing the fullness of the attributes which make God God], did not think this equality with God was a thing to be eagerly grasped or retained,"*

Walk in your NOW

Philippians 2:5, 6 AMP

Holy Spirit, I pray that you will open the mind of every readers NOW to receive everything you have put in this book to received NOW, so their minds are one with you, so you can use these words to change their NOW, changing his or her: thoughts, to change every action, renewing every habit, transforming their character to live with a Kingdom Mindset,

NOW!

In Jesus name

KNOWING YOUR SAVED

I must ask you a question. Are you saved? I will keep it very simple. I have to make sure you are saved, so you will receive every seed sown with understanding. These seeds are words that will become mighty in days to come. These words will help you become the person the Heavenly Father wants you to become! You will walk with complete confidence in the person God has called you to become NOW.

Even, if you are not saved, and do not have a relationship with Jesus, you probably still have heard of his name. It is only through Jesus that you can enjoy God's eternal promise.

> "10. *With your whole being you embrace God setting things right, and then you say it, right out loud: "God has set everything right*

Walk in your NOW

between him and me!" 11. Scripture reassures us, "No one who trusts God like this - heart and soul - will ever regret it." 12. It's exactly the same no matter what a person's religious background may be: the same God for all of us, acting the same incredibly generous way to everyone who calls out for help. 13. "Everyone who calls, 'Help, God!' gets help." 14. But how can people call for help if they don't know who to trust? And how can they know who to trust if they haven't heard of the One who can be trusted? And how can they hear if nobody tells them? 15. And how is anyone going to tell them, unless someone is sent to do it? That's why Scripture exclaims, A sight to take your breath away! Grand processions of people telling all the good things of God!" Romans 10:10-15 MS

"12. *And again, Esias saith, There shall be a root of Jesse, and he that shall rise to reign over the Gentiles; in him shall the Gentiles trust." Romans 15:12 KJV*

To become saved, you must first hear and believe in the Word of God to be the only truth. Even with all the technology, there are still some people who have not heard what Jesus has done, or even more what he is still doing on their behalf. This text gives the plan of salvation: The step is to hear the word of the Lord, believe it to be true, and then say out of your own mouth what you believe to be true. Like: ***"Jesus, I am a sinner! Forgive me; I need you Jesus, to come into my life. I want you as my Lord and Savior; I want to learn more about you."*** Now you are saved. **YES!** It is that easy.

Becoming saved is the easy part. However, what you do after accepting Christ Jesus into your life- that, my friend, is a life-long journey on earth. It is Jesus who has made you free from all sin. Jesus's blood is the reconstructioning agent bringing whosoever will believe back to right standing unto God the Father.

21. "For he hath made him to be sin for us, who knew no sin; that we might be made the righteousness of God in him." 2Corinthians 5:21 KJV

22. "And if a man have committed a sin worthy of death, and he be to be put to death, and thou hang him on a tree:" Deuteronomy 21:22 KJV

29. *"And when they had fulfilled all that was written of him, they took him down from the tree, and laid him in a sepulcher."* Acts 13:29 KJV

By Jesus hanging on a tree, becoming sin you can NOW live free from all sin. Jesus loved us all so much that He became sinful, taking all the sin of the world on Himself.

You need to know that it was not easy for Jesus to just die in your place. The trip to the hill called Calvary could have killed Him alone. It was not a cakewalk to go to that hill.

26. *"And as they led him away, they laid hold upon one Simon, a Cyrenian, coming out of the country, and on him they laid the cross, that he might bear it after Jesus."* Luke 23:26 KJV

18. *"But those things, which God before had*

shewed by the mouth of all prophets, that Christ should suffer, he hath so fulfilled." Acts 3:18 KJV

32. *"And as they came out, they found a man of Cyrene, Simon by name: him they compelled to bear his cross." Matthew 27:32 KJV*

17. *"And he bearing his cross went forth onto a place called the place of a skull, which is called in the Hebrew Golgotha:" John 19:17 KJV*

4. *"All this was done, that might be fulfilled which was spoken by the prophet, saying," Matthew 21:4 KJV*

What is sin? Sin is complete disobedience, total separation from God's will for your life. Simply put, sin is anything that keeps you from being obedient to God's perfect will for your life.

What Jesus did for you made you free from sin, and gave you right standing with God the Father. Given your eternal life in Jesus, Jesus's blood makes you righteous before God the Father on earth and in heavenly places.

Walk in your NOW

> *28. "And I give unto them eternal life; and they shall never perish, neither shall any man pluck them out of my hand." John 10:28 KJV*

When time as you know it stops, where will you spend eternity? The reason for salvation is to spend eternity in the new earth, with Christ as King. NOW you must learn who Jesus is to you.

> *"28. Come unto me, all ye that labour and are heavy laden, and I will give you rest. 29. Take my yoke upon you, and learn of me; for I am meek and lowly in heart: and ye shall find rest unto your souls. 30. For my yoke is easy, and my burden is light." Matthew 11:28-30*

When you fall in love with Jesus, you will live life with every intention to please Him for what He has done for you when He lived in the earth. He fulfilled His purpose in the earth to join humanity back unto God our heavenly Farther. Jesus' blood being shed on that hill so long along, hanging from that tree to bring any man, woman or child who believes in what He has done for them to be free from all sin.

To have a relationship with Jesus is the beginning of life everlasting; if you don't know Him it is time to get to know Jesus. Jesus is everything you need. Because of Jesus you can walk in your NOW. Knowing Jesus makes time on earth manful. Having a real relationship with Him as your Savior gives you long lasting results!

WHAT IS FAITH

Faith is a life style, not a movement. From this moment on, you will only speak words out of your mouth that you want to appear before your eyes physically.

From this day forward believe that every word you speak out of your mouth will appear before you physically. These unseen words will appear before your very eyes physically good or bad.

Your mouth will change the world you are living in NOW. I cannot tell you how important it is for you to spend time with God. It is His Spirit that will teach you how to speak seedling seeds, producing evidence of what you have spoken for His glory.

Write the words down that God speaks to you, so you can know the vision God has for your life. Use the vision He gives you to talk with Him, reminding Him of His desirers for your life in the earth, in return your only desires will become obedience to His voice, to see His word becoming physical in your life. Remind Him of the plans and purpose He has designed for you to complete for His glory. Speak those words God gives you out loud, applying words you cannot see, to frame the physical you can see. Frame the world you see with words you have spoken, so words appear before you physically.

You must believe in the words God has asked you to become, as the only truth for your life. You must put yourself aside, so you can work in the fields God will show you. Producing an abundant harvest for the Kingdom of Jesus the Christ in these last days, I believe that if you have a relationship with Jesus, you will live a life where your Heavenly Father well be will pleased.

You Now will live to please your Father. Your only desire will be to keep all of His commandments because of your love for your Heavenly Father. The covenant you and God have made with each other will be fulfilled in love.

Finally, you will keep all of these words in a secret place, believing, and applying these words to live in your NOW. You will push yourself to do the will your Father has asked you to accomplish for Him in love.

Love is the key to having wholeness in the earth and

to walk in abundance. Without LOVE you will not see God's best in the earth. As a Believer life becomes easy once we find the secrets of our creator, when you develop a relationship with Him. Spending time, talking to Him about everything, I have found out that if you spend time with God life rolls so much smoother! When we put down everything you want to do, YES!!!!!!

Once you put down everything you want to do with your lives. Then picking up the things our Lord who loves you so much, want you to do for Him, then life becomes easy! You are not yours! Your life is no longer yours to run or dictate what happens anymore! When you become a child of God given your life to Christ, He then becomes your Lord! Ok you, I know that we are not servants any more, NO, we have become Children of God through Christ given His life, fulfilling His purpose on this earth as a human! Now hope is required to see the fullness of your faith in what God has told you He will do through you, by the blood of His Son! When hope dies, your faith dies also.

As a child of God expectation is the breeding ground for miracles! When you fail to expect or believe that God is and will always be, He can't work for you, or through you! Your faith has then failed to deliver the will of God for your life! Take the time and write down what you expect from God by doing His will on earth, make it plan, and thank God for doing what you wrote now, thank Him unto you see it here on earth manifested, you have to ask Him 1st what He want you to do!

Yes this is how you release your faith, talking to God or praying, then writing it down, keeping it in a place you go to pray, and whenever you think about it give thanks to God for bring it to pass in your life. Even if it hasn't manifested yet give thanks, and when it has manifested, because we are on God's time not ours still thank Him for doing it! Faith is the substance of things hoped for,

> *Now Faith is the substance of things hoped for, the evidence of things not seen. Hebrews 11:1"*

Your Hope in God working on your behalf this enables you to see the fullness of your Faith that He is your source! Hope is earnest, heartfelt, favorable, confident expectation; it's a desirable goal from God's Word. It's expecting with an outstretched hand looking for what you believe will happen with God help.

Walk in your NOW

Hope will change and rearrange your plans. If you could only believe me, If I was you I would put my entire plan, the life I wanted aside and then ask God what do you want me to do! I need it clear and plan so I can do your will for my life, being you are my Lord!

If I could get you to believe, even though we are sons now through Christ, we need, and should want to be His servants! Then He will make a covenant with you, as long as you do what He what you to, the way He said do it! Without understanding of your covenant with Christ, you won't have hope,

> *"That we should be to the praise of His glory, who first trusted in Christ. In whom you also trusted, after that you heard the word of truth, the gospel of your salvation: in whom also after that you believed, you were sealed with that holy Spirit of promise. Ephesians 2:12-13"*

Hope is required for your faith to work! Scriptures are essential to our hope! Through patience and comfort in the scriptures we have hope,

> *"For whatsoever things were written aforetime were written for our learning, that we through patience and comfort of the scriptures might have hope. Roman 15:4"*

> *"My soul faints for Your salvation: but I hope in Your Word…….. You are my hiding place and my shield: I hope in Your word. Psalm 119: 81,114"*

I pray that you will see all you hope comes from the Word of God, having a relationship with Him spending quietly time with Him. The objective of spending time in the Word is to develop hope in your heart, if you are not spending time in the Word, you will not be able to develop hope! It is sad to say that some of my Father's kids don't make time for Him; they are too busy to spend time with their God. I like to ask you this what if God did you like you do Him? I pray that you hope hasn't died; don't allow delay to cause you to lose hope. See what I have found is that the delay make you depend on Him more once you have really gotten real with Him, and doing what He wants you to do, not what you want! Delay is not denial.

I have seen with me, my delay is because of me

putting His will off for my life for so long! This is me; it might be different for you though! See for me He still talks and bless me for being obedient, not just the big one yet! He is preparing me for them! Hope postponed makes the heart sick,

> *Hope deferred makes the heart sick: but when the desire comes, it is a tree. Proverbs 13:12"*

That tree from God will produce much fruit! This is way my heart sickness is no more because He is and I know He has already completed my life in chapter 1, now it is just unfolding before my eyes, according to my obedience to His Word. My beloved brethren I pray you this, **Expectation is the breeding ground for miracles**! You have to believe that, it is done then give thanks constantly! Constantly give thanks! Even if it has not manifested yet! Give thanks! Thanks Him CONSTANTLY! Remain in expectation of what you desire to come to pass through Gods will for your life!

The man at the gate called Beautiful was in expectation of receiving something, he had an outstretched hand wanting to receive, **Act 1-7.** Now look at God, He did above all he could ask or think! We have to expect, without it what will fuel your hope? This man walked immediately because he had such great expectation! Peter and John also had great expectation that the man would walk as well! I challenge you to try my Father! He even asks you to try Him and see how **GOOD** He really is!

If you would Get Real with yourself, letting go of everything you are trying to do! And then turning to the wall and asking God *"What must I do? You have put me here for this time in this season what do you have me to do to leave an impact of a servant's heart!"* Write down what you have heard from God to do!

Now you are expecting God to do it, make it public, and immediately thank God for it! Thanksgiving is confident hope which expands your capacity to receive from God in your life on earth! That the secret **Thanksgiving makes your faith capacity expand** so, LETS GET REAL and be about our Fathers business!

Walk in your NOW

APPLYING YOUR FAITH

How will you fulfill your life purpose NOW? You must walk in the divine will God has planned for your life's enjoyment in the earth. The only way you can please God is by faith. If you do not have faith it is impossible to please God, you must believe that God is.

> *"6. But without faith it is impossible to please Him, for he who comes to God must believe that He is, and that He is a rewarder of those who diligently seek Him." Hebrews 11:6 KJV*

When I heard that I cannot please God without faith, I wondered what the method of obtaining this faith is. I wonder what was it I needed to have faith in. The foundation or this faith is, to believe in what Jesus did and now doing on your behalf. I am sorry faith is not a deeper understanding then that, you must believe in Jesus or you just really, do not have faith at all. I have repeatedly heard, "Faith comes by hearing, and hearing by the Word of God." So that tells me I have to hear something, spoken by someone.

> *"17. Consequently, faith comes from hearing the message, and the message is heard through the word of Christ." Romans 10:17 NIV*

This did not say I had faith, it only said faith comes by being spoken. Once you hear something you must earthier believe it or not believe it. If you believe what you have heard, then something else has to take place. You then think or mediate on what you have believed. Mediating on what you believe creates a thought patron, the thought patron creates actions, and actions make habits. I have always analyzed everything because I look for any possible loopholes in everything.

I was one of those who had to see it to believe it before I believed it. I analyzed everything because it was hard for me to trust anyone, or believe in anything anyone said to be true. When I started to read Gods' Living Word, and applying Gods' Living Words, laws and principles to my life daily I started seeing thing change in my life.

The law I used most was the spoken word, the principle I used was to believe in what I said to be the only truth, with the proper intense corresponding actions following what I believed in. I sow, and still seeing lasting results. I was not fully converted then though. Being my life NOW is lived in pleasing God. I need you to understand, that what you say will appear before you physically.

"50. Jesus answered and said to him, "Because I said to you, 'I saw you under the fig tree,' do you believe? You will see greater things than these." John 1:50 NKJV

'12. If I tell you things that are plain as the hand before your face and you don't believe me, what use is there in telling you of things you can't see, the things of God?" John 3:12 MSG

"48. Jesus told him, "Unless you [people] see signs and wonders, you will not believe." John 4:48

CSB

You know what is funny. Even though I was not sold out God still keep His word. With my doubtful thinking, God has proven to me that I could trust in His Living Word to be absolute truth. God showed me some things about Himself that I could not question or fight to prove He is a God that loves me where I was. He proved to me that I could count on Him no matter how things appeared in the natural. He proved He is faithful all He need was me was to believe in Him.

I was hard to trust Him without always seeing or even understanding how He would do it. That was the human in me, once I have truly believed in god being sold out, I NOW understand how believe in what God has told me to be the truth; I came to this understanding when I decided to truly please God with my whole life! It took time for me to do this, like it will take time for you to as well. What it really took was for me to just believe!

God allowed me to try Him; all He wanted was for me to simply believe in Him, without doubting. I learned to trust in God no matter how my circumstances appeared. Patience had to work her perfect work in me.

I learned to trust in what God told me, more then

what I could physically see. He proved to me I could trust Him without doubting in His ability to be my God. He knew I would need to spend time with Him so He could talk to me. When I spent time with him he told me what to do, to really see His Living Word appear before me physically. He fulfills my every need, with Him.

What He showed me was that I did not have to find loop holes anymore because all He wanted was to love me. I still tried to find loop holes because if faith did not work, I would tell the world not to believe in faith or God.

I studied and studied faith until God gave me an understanding of what faith is. God had a plan for me, so I had to understand faith to give a understanding to you NOW. This will allow you to trust Him without doubting, once you believe.

God is. That is the big secret! God told Moses to tell them I am sent you! God is whatever you need Him to be, when you need him to be!

> *"14. And God said unto Moses, I AM THAT I AM: and he said, Thus shalt thou say unto the children of Israel, I AM hath sent me unto you."*
> *Exodus 3:14 KJV*

God is NOW preparing you to have complete confidence in Him being with you, in your life! God said He will never leave you are for sake you.

> *"5. Don't be obsessed with getting more material things. Be relaxed with what you have. Since God assured us, "I'll never let you down, never walk off and leave you," Hebrews 13:5 MSG*

God want us to be in love with Him, He is your Heavenly Father. Think about it, if your earthly parent or parents took care of you every need. How much more can God do, being He is God? When you grab on to God and spend time with him in His Living Word. God will show you His plans for your life on earth. If you could truly try Him, taking God at His word only He can tell you what your life on earth will become.

To walk in your NOW take you taking God for His word. Living in faith, knowing God is.

NOW FAITH

God wanted me to become a servant first, and then He would develop me to live in sonship. Therefore, God showed me faith. If you can grasp these words, they will change your life forever. You have read these words before; you might be able to quote them.

I speak, "to your mind, mind be open and hear what the Lord wants you to hear. Mind receives these words as thoughts so God can use them more effectively." In Jesus name

> "1. NOW FAITH is the substance of things hoped for, the evidence of things not seen. 2. For by it elders obtained a good report. 3. Through faith we understand that the worlds were framed by the word of God, so that

things which are seen were not made of things which do appear." Hebrews 11:1-3 KJV

Reading this made me start to think. If I could not please God without faith, I needed to understand what faith means. I understood that spoken words play a very important part in faith. If speaking plays a major part in this faith walk, I had to learn how to believe in the words that were coming out my mouth as truth. I decided to do some research. I discovered that:

FAITH: Is allegiance to duty of a person; fidelity to ones' promises.

SUBSTANCE: Is ultimate reality that underlies all outward manifestation and change; practical importance.

HOPE: Is to desire with expectation of obtainment; to expect with confidence, fulfillment.

EVIDENCE: Is something that furnishes proof, to prove a fact by proving other events; circumstances which afford a base is of or reasonable.

SEEN. Seen deals with the five senses, things that can be senses in the physical.

With a better understanding of the meaning of faith, I

re-read *Hebrews 11:1-3* with a more open mind. I am going to plug the definitions into the passage in red.

*Now **(my allegiance and duty of God)** is the **(ultimate reality that underlies all outward manifestation and change, practical importance)** of things **(to desire with expectation of obtainment; to expect with confidence, or fulfillment)**, the **(word of God furnishes proof, to prove a fact by proving other events circumstances which afford abase is reasonable)** of **(words spoken out of my mouth)** not seen, for by **(allegiance and duty to Jesus)** elders **(people before us that trusted in God)** obtained a good report. Through **(their allegiance and duty to God)** we understand that worlds were framed by the Word of God, so that things which are seen were not made of things which do appear.*

I knew then that the words that come out of my mouth frames physical worlds around me, because I am made in the image of God, I am made in His likeness.

This changed my life. This framed the way I talk forever. I have learned to only speak and think words that I want to appear before me physically. If I think something not in the will of God, I NOW speak Gods' Living Word to that Thought. I remembered that God framed everything we see with words, He spoke out loud. I have seen the manifestation of the power of God's spoken words. He said that I am made in His likeness. You are also made in His likeness.

Jesus said, "Greater things will they do that believe." Believe you can do greater things than Jesus has done in the earth, when you believe. I have changed my speech forever and I have changed my thought patterns as well.

> *12. I tell you the truth, anyone who has faith in me will do what I have been doing. He will do even greater things than these, because I am going to the Father. John 14:12 NIV*

It is time when the true sons of God will stand and use this God given power to reframe this world we live in, We must frame it back the way God has intended it to be. Jesus is on His way back, He is going to trust we have done what He asked us to do.

Who are the sons of God?

"13. For if you live according to the sinful nature, you will die; but if by the Spirit you put to death the misdeeds of the body, you will live, 14. because those who are led by the Spirit of God are sons of God. 15. For you did not receive a spirit that makes you a slave again to fear, but you received the Spirit of sonship. And by him we cry, ""Abba," Father." 16. The Spirit himself testifies with our spirit that we are God's children." Romans 8:13-16 NIV

"24. even us, whom he also called, not only from the Jews but also from the Gentiles? 25. As he says in Hosea: "I will call them 'my people' who are not my people; and I will call her 'my loved one' who is not my loved one," 26. and, "It will happen that in the very place where it was said to them, 'You are not my people,' they will be called 'sons of the living God.' " 27. Isaiah cries out concerning Israel: "Though the number of the Israelites be *like the sand by the sea, only the remnant will be saved. 28. For the Lord will carry out his sentence on earth with speed and finality." Romans 9:24-28 NIV*

The sons of God are mature believe in the Lord Jesus the Christ, that will walk with power, as Jesus showed when He walked on the earth. They will move with POWER from up high, being led by the Holy Spirit as Jesus was lead as He walked the earth, so all believers' even unbelievers will see the true power of the one and only true living God Jesus, working in the earth.

WALK IN YOUR NOW

Let us talk about how you will become what your Heavenly Father wants you to become. Know that Jesus loves you no matter what you have done, are doing, or will do. Jesus will never stop loving you.

> *"16. For God so loved the world, that he gave his only begotten Son, that whosoever believeth in him should not perish, but have everlasting life."* John 3:16 KJV

There is a heaven and a hell; they both exist. There is a real devil, and he wants your soul. The devil's job is to steal, kill, and destroy. His greatest trick is convincing people that there is no heaven or hell. His plan was to get you to think sin is just having fun. Know that Jesus gave His life for your freedom, so you can have everlasting life in Him.

Jesus came to give your life, so you can enjoy a life with abundance on earth. If you choose to live an obedient life in the earth for Jesus, you will enjoy a lasting, full life till it runs over with peace, love, joy and true happiness. Once you step into eternity with Jesus in heaven, to live on the new earth you will hear Him say how well pleased He is with His good and faithful servant.

> *"28. Even as the Son of man came not to be ministered unto, but to minister, and to give his life a ransom for many." Matthew 20:28 KJV*

You will have a life of abundance with Jesus. Your life will overflow with love. People will become attracted to what your Father is doing through you in your new life of obedience to the Holy Spirit.

Your life will become a magnet to people who will want to know the one true God for whom you NOW live for. People will want to have a real relationship with Him, as you NOW have with Jesus.

> *"3. The LORD hath appeared of old unto me, saying, Yea, I have loved thee with an everlasting love: therefore with loving kindness have I drawn thee."* Jeremiah 31:3 KJV

> *"32. And I, if I be lifted up from the earth, will draw all men unto me"* John 12:32 KJV

Filling your heart up with false hope and no substance is not the intent of this book. You must know that if you really live for Jesus, your life has changed. The Heavenly Father will only put in your hands what you have proven to Him you can handle for His Kingdom.

> *"21. That I may cause those that love me to inherit substance; and I will fill their treasures."* Proverbs 8:21 KJV

> *"42. Jesus said unto them, If God were your Father, ye would love me: for I proceeded forth and came from God; neither came I of myself, but he sent me."* John 8:42 KJV

> *"21. He that hath my commandments, and keepeth them, he it is that loveth me: and he that loveth me shall be loved of my Father, and I will love him, and will manifest myself to him." John 14:21 KJV*

Your Father will not put anything in your hands or life that will take His place in your life. God wants you to need Him in everything you do. He wants you to always seek Him before you make any decision for your life in the earth.

> *"132. Look thou upon me, and be merciful unto me, as thou usest to do unto those that love thy name." Psalm 119:132 KJV*

> *"17. I love them that love me; and those that seek me early shall find me." Proverbs 8:17 KJV*

Your Father desires for you to obey Him. He loves an obedient child. Your obedience to His Spirit with the currency He has allowed you to obtain is how He makes sure He can trust you with lasting riches, and wealth to possess in the earth. He desires to put riches in your hands to use for His Kingdom to have might, drawing unbelieving as well as believers unto Him through you.

If your motive is to seek and please God with all you possess, when your desirer is to live with a Kingdom Mindset; there is nothing the Lord will not bless for you to use to give glory to the Kingdom of God. Showing how much Jesus loves you, living a life full of fulfillment.

Jesus loves you so much He gave His life so you can enjoy life on earth. Jesus love is unconditional, He loves the whole world.

> *15. Love not the world, neither the things that are in the world. If any man love the world, the love of the Father is not in him. 16. For all that is in the world, the lust of the eyes, and the pride of life, is not of the Father, but is of the world. 17. And the world passeth away, and the lust thereof: but he that doeth the will of God abideth forever. 1 John 2:15-17*

Jesus wants you to know if you are trusting in the

things of the world, they all will pass away only the Kingdom of God will last. That's why Jesus gave His life so you and every believer will have everlasting life in Him. This is the allotment love; there is no greater love then Jesus love for you NOW.

Walk in your NOW

THE PLAN THAT WORKS

There are seven basics principle you should know and live by to enjoy a life of true fulfillment in the earth. You have to seek God first in everything you do, seeking to really have a relationship with the Lord Jesus. You're seeking God to tell you His plans and vision for your life. This is really the only way you will have lasting peace on earth.

Every time a man truly sloth after a relationship with God; God allowed them to find him and He gave them instruction to save humanity, to bring mankind back until Him.

These are seven basic things needing to start a life of true and lasting fulfillment on the earth:

1. Seek God with all your whole heart.

> "33. But seek ye first the kingdom of God, and his righteousness; and all these things shall be added unto you."

Matthew 6:33 KJV

2. You have to desire change. You must want to change into what God desires for you to become.

> *"24. Then said Jesus unto his disciples, If any man will come after me, let him deny himself, and take up his cross, and follow me." Matthew 16:24 KJV*

3. You have to allow God to heal you completely in mind, body, and soul. You will receive emotional, physical, and spiritual healing.

> *"22. But Jesus turned him about, and when he saw her, he said, Daughter, be of good comfort; thy faith hath made thee whole. And the woman was made whole from that hour." Matthew 9:22 KJV*

4. You must move forward, forgetting the things you have done in the past. The past is behind you. God forgave you. Now forgive yourself.

Walk in your NOW

> "*14. I press toward the mark for the prize of the high calling of God in Christ Jesus.*" *Philippians 3:14 KJV*

5. You must have no fear. God has not given you a spirit of fear, but of power, love, a sound mind, with self-control.

> "*7. For God hath not given us the spirit of fear; but of power, and of love, and of a sound mind.*" *2 Timothy 1:7 KJV*

6. You must walk in forgiveness. How can God forgive your trespassing, if you do not forgive others who trespass against you?

> "*15. But if ye forgive not men their trespasses, neither will your Father forgive your trespasses.*" *Matthew 6:15 KJV*

7. You must remain faithful to the vision. Stay focused on the promises of God. You will see God's Word appear right before your eyes.

> *2. "And the LORD answered me, and said, Write the vision, and make it plain upon tables, that he may run that readeth it." Habakkuk 2:2 KJV*

To know your true purpose in the earth, you must have a relationship with the Jesus. Then you will know what your place is in your Heavenly Fathers Kingdom. You will have true enjoyment with abundance, enjoying a fulfilling life in the earth, completing your purpose in the earth for your Heavenly Father to be well pleased.

I know I want to hear him tell me the day He returns, and call me to meet Him in the sky, this is my son in whom I am well pleased. My life NOW is lived to spend eternity in the new earth with Jesus as my Lord and King!

The plan that works is to spend time seeking God with you whole heart, not seeking Him for what He can do for you. God wants you to seek Him because of the love He has showed you, because you want to enjoy him as your King for ever more! Know God knows you better then you can ever think you know yourself, so you can play games with Him. He is whetting on you to truly take Him at His word.

WHAT GOD WANTS

Every success in life is based on the strength of your prayer life, what you believe in, your everyday actions. Prayer is a necessary discipline in the life of every Believer because it authorizes God to get involved with our situations and circumstances. What I've found out is that every believer outside the USA has this discipline and walk in it with their whole heart! Wanting God to give them lasting instruction, I pray you find time to talk with God.

How can you have a relationship with someone and not spend time with them? God loves it when you spend time with him studying, reading, and talking with Him. The most powerful thing any human can do is pray in faith. Spending time with God awaiting His divine instruction to execute in the earth is what every believer must do.

To see true abundance you must spend time in the presence of the living God; spending time with God is a vital part of learning about whom you are to Him: studying and reading His written Word, seeking to know His written Word, is how you become a lintel weapon for the Kingdom of God.

To know Gods' written Word with the help and guidance of the Holy Spirit is how you will know the real truth. By spending time with Him, Your desires will change into God's desires for your life. You will become what God intends for you to become for his glory.

"32. People who don't know God and the way he works fuss over these things, but you know both God and how he works. 33. Steep your life in God-reality, God-initiative, God-provisions. Don't worry about missing out. You'll find all your everyday human concerns will be met. 34. "Give your entire attention to what God is doing right now, and don't get worked up about what may or may not happen tomorrow. God will help you deal with whatever hard things come up when the time comes." Matthew 6:32-34 MSG

Walk in your NOW

> *"30. For all these things do the nations of the world seek after: and your Father knoweth that ye have need of these things. 31. But rather seek ye the kingdom of God; and all these things shall be added unto you. 32. Fear not, little flock; for it is your Father's good pleasure to give you the kingdom. Luke 12:30-32 KJV*

What has God said to you, about who you are to Him? Have you written what God has told you down? What is keeping you from becoming what god said?

Spending time with God, reading His Word will give your faith assurance. Spending time with God will help you to develop a stronger trust in the Living Word of God working on your behalf. Spending time with God creates a strong foundation and understanding in God's plan for your life in the earth. Believing in God's Word gives lasting hope. Once you spend time with God reading, studying, and meditating on the Living Word of God.

The Holy Spirit will give you detail instruction; you will have to act upon the divine instruction the Holy

Spirit gives with your whole heart. Your intense corresponding action must show you trust and belief in what God has told you. Know you will find true peace in what Jesus did for you; to return unto God the Father because of Jesus you NOW can live a life of wholeness, where you are complete in the Father and the Son, were the Holy Spirit leads you daily.

> *7. "For there are three that bear record in heaven, the Father, the Word, and the Holy Ghost: and these three are one." 1 John 5:7 KJV*

> *10. "He who receives you receives me, and he who receives me receives the one who sent me." Matthew 10:40 NIV*

You can develop serene confidence in the power of the Holy Spirit working with you, knowing He works through you as long as you obey. The Holy Spirit can only give life to the Living Word of God you've obtained thought spending time with God; the Living Word of God applied to your thinking strengthen your belief in the power of God working in you, so you can use God's spoken word to frame worlds around you.

Believeth in the Living word of God needs to have intense corresponding actions to see lasting power working on your behalf in life on earth!

You can be filled with the Holy Spirit, having power from on high once you have believed in the name of Jesus, being born again choosing to allow the Holy Spirit to live in your heart.

Choosing to do the work Jesus started, allows the Holy Spirit to lead you into all truth. The power of the Holy Spirit will come upon you, as you are doing the will of God for your life! The Holy Spirit gives the power needed to destroy the works of the devil as you continue the works Jesus started!

> 22. *"[I Will Put My Spirit Within You] "Therefore say to the house of Israel, Thus says the Lord GOD: It is not for your sake, O house of Israel, that I am about to act, but for the sake of my holy name, which you have profaned among the nations to which you came." Ezekiel 36:22 ESV*

> *11. "I baptize you with water for repentance, but the One who is coming after me is more powerful than I. I am not worthy to take off His sandals. He Himself will baptize you with the Holy Spirit and fire." Matthew 3:11 CSB*

Being born again is truly allowing the Holy Spirit to change the way you process thing, making your thoughts and action to align with God's plans for your life. You will never know the true power that is in you until you spend time with God, allowing Him to speak to you.

The only way to find perfect peace is to know God, knowing what He has created you to do for Him in the earth. Let me ask you why not spend time with God? As your talking with God, you are allowing Him access to your life to show the power that is within you.

To have a Kingdom Mindset takes you really seeking God. If the world you live in NOW is not bringing you peace, develop a prayer life talk to God, He will talk back if you let Him. Prayer is you and God one on one conversing about your life. God wants you to Commune with him on a daily bases. I challenge you if you really want to know the investment God has made in you;

spend time with Him allow His Spirit to teach you all truth.

Life as you know it will not be the same. What you must do is make time for God to really exist in your life. God wants to have a more intense relationship then just: New Year's Eve, Easter, and Christmas. God has so much for you to do the only way you will ever have peace is to make Him truly God over your life.

Once you allow a relationship with God to be established you will really see the co-creating power that lives inside of you come forward. God's power is in you and He is waiting on you to uses it for His glory!

UNFORGIVENESS

There are two ways to keep the perfect love of God out of your life. One is by not believing in what Jesus has done on your behalf. The other is unforgiveness. If you do not believe in Jesus being the only way, what have you built your faith in?

> *13. "You can enter God's Kingdom only through the narrow gate. The highway to hell is broad, and its gate is wide for the many who choose the easy way." Matthew 7:13 NLT*

> *6. "Jesus answered, "I am the way and the truth and the life. No one comes to the Father except through me." John 14:6 NIV*

The most vital hindrance and number one thing that will stop you from seeing any of the promise of God for your life is unforgiveness. Your old thoughts tell you it is

Walk in your NOW

hard to forgive because of the pain and the hurt you felt. Once you allow the Spirit of God to heal you, the pain, hurt will not have anything to hold on to, having a Kingdom Mindset you know that God has forgiven you; so no matter what the offence is you have to forgive.

It's funny when we as humans are offended, hurt or simply done wrong. Only the one that has choose to hold on to the pain is affected. The person that infected the pain has already moved on. They do not hold on to their wrong doings. Jesus said one time we should forgive no matter what the offence.

I know this sounds hard, however I am here to tell you can forgive. See to have lasting peace you cannot allow anything keep you from Gods' perfect peace. It has been proven time and time again that the only person being hinder from any wrong doing is the one that has choose to hold on to the wrong doing.

Once you know that God has given you the power over every pain, then you activate Gods' love you have victory. Most people wrong other out of spite, or just plain ignorance. Most are just repeating the cycle of pain, because they were heart. Know Jesus died for every wrong doing, every pain to not have any power over you.

No matter what, unforgiveness is NOW in your past! The love of God has NOW removed: all pain, all rejection, even the bitterness, the love of God has removed them taking them up from the very root so the.

From today on know you have the power and the way you felt in your past, is no more! No longer will you react to any pain, any hurt, or any bitterness the same way. Once you have face it, then given your agreement to the Holy Spirit it is NO MORE!

> 28. *"This is my blood of the covenant, which is poured out for many for the forgiveness of sins." Matthew 26:28 NIV*

> 17. *"This is what you are to say to Joseph: I ask you to forgive your brother's the sins and the wrongs they committed in treating you so badly.' Now please forgive the sins of the servants of the God of your father." When their message came to him, Joseph wept" Genesis 50:17 NIV*

> 34. *"then hear from heaven and forgive the sin of your people Israel and bring them back to the land you gave to their fathers." 1 Kings 8:34 NIV*

14. For if you forgive men when they sin against you, your heavenly Father will also forgive you." Matthew 6:14 NIV

15. "But if you do not forgive men their sins, your Father will not forgive your sins." Matthew 6:15 NIV

Say this out loud, "I am free from all pain, all rejection, and all bitterness. Because of the blood of Jesus, I'm free; No longer will I entertain any: pain, bitterness, or rejection. Holy Spirit uproots every root of pain, bitterness, and rejection, and burns them all to ashes, removing every root of pain, rejection, and bitterness from me NOW, In the Name of Jesus.

Through the power of the blood of Jesus, you are free! Ok I hear you, yes when the adversary try to bring back an old memory, will you react the same way. NO, see the one of the tricks the devil uses is trying to get you to remember your past. NOW, you have been freed the Holy Spirit has removed the old reaction. Your new reaction is to love, even more to love them that try to hurt you. They themselves are in pain and in need to meet the power of Gods' forgiveness themselves. You will show them Gods love because you have let every pain, and or wrong doing go, you are free because you let them all go NOW. Nothing from this day forward will keep you from walking in the love of Jesus. Your only desire is to imitate Christ love, because you have the mind of Christ NOW. Enjoy the abundant life Jesus' blood has given you NOW.

Every time you are reminded of your past you must speak to those thoughts! YES, you must speak to those thoughts, out loud with the Living Word of God! This way you will no longer think about the past hurt. Speaking to those thoughts, gives the Holy Spirit the promotion to intervene on your behalf.

Using Gods creative power given to you to frame worlds, use it to also renew your way of thinking removing every seed, or deed of hurt from your past speaking to them with the Living Word of God. Speaking to the thought this is an intense corresponding action of your faith in the power that works within you. The power is in you; use the power to have peace.

The words you are reading are seeds the Holy Spirit has planted into my heart to share with you NOW. He inspired me to write these words so you can see them in this book. You must believe these words to be truth for your life.

The Holy Spirit has applied these words to your heart to empower your new Kingdom Mindset, to recognize the power of spoken words. God's words will appear before your eyes physically! Your hope will become evidence which will enable you to speak God's Word aloud and produce physical results.

THE INVESTMENT

Since you are NOW set free from all sin, you cannot help but to fall even deeper in love with Jesus the Christ. Knowing how to make investments is very important in life on the earth. Knowing how to make the right Kingdom investments, not being emotionally leaded is vital for your return on the investment in the earth. Let the Holy Spirit lead you in every investment on the earth, be it your time, your money, let the Holy Spirit lead you.

Only then can you be assured a lasting result from your obedience to the Holy Spirit leading you in your earthly endeavors to have eternal results.

When you make an investment in the world, you expect a return on your investment right? You will also have a return when making Kingdom investments, be it with your money, and or your time. Every right investment will have an expected return in the natural; likewise the right investment will have an expected return spiritually as well.

I am saddened to tell you every bad investment being emotionally lead, will not have a return natural or spiritually. If you gave money as a seed or offering, not being led by the Holy Spirit, there is no expected return. How do you know the difference between a right and wrong investment? If you are investing your money naturally, you must investigate what you are about to invest in. What is your expected return, even more how long before you see your expected return from your investment?

Money is not everything, however it dose pay the bills and get you what you want. Money is a tool; money should be governed by rules. Money is dose not bring happiness, however it can give you a natural peace. You should control you money, not money controlling you. Falling in love with money is a place where you don't want to be, money comes and goes. Learn how to live within your means, my friend this is how you control money. Money finds a way to control you once you start living be on your means. Always wanting more is a bad place to be.

> *"5. Your life should be free from the love of money. Be satisfied with what you have, for He Himself has said, I will never leave you or forsake you."* Hebrews 13:5 CSB

If you really love God, you are seeking Him because you are so in love with Him. You are not seeking God because of what He can do; know God knows your heart. Your desire should be to know your God your Father more intimately. Jesus said seek the righteousness of God, not money or things.

I did not say money is bad, no; the love of money is the root to all evil. If you fall in love with Jesus, you are consciously keeping His commandments; you are choosing to obey the Holy Spirit. This is my friend is the key to experience true lasting wealth in the earth. You have to know why you are allowed to gain wealth, even more once you have it what to do with it.

The only reason God has, and will entrust riches and wealth into your hands is to establish our far Father's covenant. This was a covenant the Lord God made with Abram our far father, because Abram made God, his God. No matter what God always keeps His promises, if He said it must come to pass.

Walk in your NOW

"17. You may say to yourself, "My power and the strength of my hands have produced this wealth for me." 18. But remember the LORD your God, for it is he who gives you the ability to produce wealth, and so confirms his covenant, which he swore to your forefathers, as it is today. 19. If you ever forget the LORD your God and follow other gods and worship and bow down to them, I testify against you today that you will surely be destroyed. 20. Like the nations the LORD destroyed before you, so you will be destroyed for not obeying the LORD your God." Deuteronomy 8:17-20

Seeing true wealth, you have to desire to establish God's covenant in the earth. When you make an investment with a pure heart being led by the Holy Spirit, expect to have a great return. When you invest, you should allow the Holy Spirit to lead you. Only the Holy Spirit can position you to reap a great return in God's proper time.

"7. So that neither the planter is anything,

nor the waterier; but God the giver of the increase." 1 Corinthians 3:7 DBY

"7. [Let] each man [do] according as he hath purposed in his heart: not grudgingly, or of necessity: for God loveth a cheerful giver." 2 Corinthians 9:7 ASV

A lot of time we want it NOW. Today people are in this microwave mentality, wanting everything at their own convince. Remember God knows every thought you have before you have it. We are not our own any more, we must relearn to do thing when God says, God knows the best time for you to see your return. God is not in time as we know it, He sees and knows all because He is not on a time line like our lives are.

God looks at your faith, your heart, and your intent when you sow seeds. We have to come to the place where we use money the right way! The only way to do that is to first have a relationship with Him, then obeying His Spirit. When you invest have good intent and the right motive so Gods' Spirit will see fit for a proper return.

"6. And this: He who is sowing sparingly,

> *sparingly also shall reap; and he who is sowing in blessings, in blessings also shall reap; 7. each one, according as he doth purpose in heart, not out of sorrow or out of necessity, for a cheerful giver doth God love, 8. and God [is] able all grace to cause to abound to you, that in everything always all sufficiency having, ye may abound to every good work," 2 Corinthians 9:6-8*

Think of it like this, one year to us is like one day to God. If you do not see your investment lead by the Holy Spirit on this side of glory, it is waiting for you in the Heaven when you meet Jesus. You will enjoy every investment you have sown in the new earth. Gods' promises are eternal so Gods' time is not controlled by time as we know it.

> *"3. You tell us to return to what we were; you change us back to dust. 4. A thousand years to you are like one day; they are like yesterday, already gone, like a short hour in the night. 5. You carry us*

> *away like a flood; we last no longer than a dream. We are like weeds that sprout in the morning"* Psalm 90:3-5

Your Heavenly Father has made an investment in you, every day your eyes open and you wake up on the earth. Our Heavenly Father has made an investment for the whole world, by the name of Jesus our Christ. When will God see His return from what He has invested in the world, even more when He see a return from His investment in you?

> *16. "For God loved the world so much that he gave his only Son, so that everyone who believes in him may not die but have eternal life"* John 3:16 GNTA

You control the time it takes for God to see His return in what He has invested in you. Your Heavenly Father sees His return through your believeth in what Jesus did, it is a bonus when you are obedience to the Holy Spirits' guidance.

God sent His only Son into the earth as an investment for many children to come His one investment. His investment was to send His begotten Son to give up His own life, to make all that will believe in Jesus' action being leaded by the Holy Spirit to make us all free from every sin. He invested Jesus so we could be with Him in eternity, making us righteous and holy because He loves us that much.

God invested His best, Jesus. God wants to have many sons, as a return of Him investing His only son Jesus. You are His child, yes, you once you believe and are born again.

> *"12. He did not enter by means of the blood of goats and calves; but he entered the Most Holy Place once for all by his own blood, having obtained eternal redemption. 13. The blood of goats and bulls and the ashes of a heifer sprinkled on those who are ceremonially unclean sanctify them so that they are outwardly clean. 14. How much more, then, will the blood of Christ, who through the eternal Spirit offered himself unblemished to God, cleanse our consciences from acts that lead to death, so that we may serve the living God! 15. For this reason Christ is the mediator of a new covenant, that those who*

are called may receive the promised eternal inheritance--now that he has died as a ransom to set them free from the sins committed under the first covenant. 16. In the case of a will, it is necessary to prove the death of the one who made it, 17. because a will is in force only when somebody has died; it never takes effect while the one who made it is living. 18. This is why even the first covenant was not put into effect without blood." Hebrews 9:12-19 NIV

Since you have read to this point, you are really growing stronger knowing you are Gods' child. Allow God to see the return He placed in you, is all God ever wanted. Being obedient to God's Spirit, God receive the honor from your life in the earth. By obeying the Holy Spirit you will be living a life where God the Father can be well pleased with you His child in the earth.

If you are living for riches, you will never obtain enough riches to ever make you happy, or to give you peace. You will want more and more until you reach a point where, all you seek are the riches of this world missing out Gods' best. You will find yourself turning away from God's perfect plan for your life. Your whole life NOW will become where you are seeking after a mirage, sad thing is you will never find fulfillment in the earth.

Beginning today, riches will seek you! Your thoughts will become a well of ideas to obtain wealth! Numerous ideas will come to your mind. Your hands are blessed to create these ideas to become physical, because you are seeking God's righteousness in everything you do. God will add things to you with no sorrow.

> 5. *"And the Lord confirmed the realm in his hand; and all Judah gave gifts to Jehoshaphat, and riches without number, and much glory was made to him." 2 Chronicles 17:5 WYC*

When God gives you the thoughts, you will seek Him in how to bless Him with what He has given you. Men will give you riches because the Lord will put it in their hearts!

Your new Kingdom Mindset is growing. As you seek God's righteousness, your mind is being renewed at an accelerant rate like never before because of your obedience to the guidance from the Holy Spirit. Seeking God in everything you do, glorifying God with your life has become your Kingdom Mindset NOW.

> *28. "Are you tired? Worn out? Burned out on religion? Come to me. Get away with me and you'll recover your life. I'll show you how to take a real rest. 29. Walk with me and work with me - watch how I do it. Learn the unforced rhythms of grace. I won't lay anything heavy or ill-fitting on you. 30. Keep company with me and you'll learn to live freely and lightly." Matthew 11:28-31 MSG*

You have made up your own mind to follow Jesus, and the Holy Spirit is keeping you from the hands of all wickedness in the earth. You will make your Father happy, giving Him the full return He wants from your life NOW.

My Father wants you to be wealthy, and not just so we can have a better life on earth. The primary purpose for wealth is to establish God's covenant on the earth by man! Most think that prosperity is just about money, it involves money; however money is more of a fuel, money will show all who you really are.

God needs you whole in every area of your life; you have to become an obedient child to God. You must want to be complete, you have to agree with God and then do

Walk in your NOW

your part! You have to agree with in the will that our Father has for your lives. I'm not saying everyone will be millionaire, your social status depends on the purpose God has for you to fulfill for Him. By becoming obedient to His every word, speaking your faith in what He has done. Your social status doses have a price! Our lasting social status depends on God's purpose, He designed you to do something only you can fulfill for Him. What is that?

Know our Father has put in your heart, what He wants. Your obedience to the Holy Spirit ill detriment your social statues in your life and in the Kingdom of God. What has the most power in the earth is currency, money! If you show God you Him, He will show you He trust you with it as well. He has put in your heart, a desire that drives you to fulfill. God wants you whole in every area of your life!

Prosperity is not objective of doing well with physical worldly thing, the thing are given because of LOVE! Prosperity means to exceed or to deal wisely.

Prosperity includes: Lasting Healing, Whole Deliverance, Truth of Salvation and the world POWER, money!

The purpose of prosperity is to establish our for

fathers' promise with God the Lord! The covenant in the earth God made is for God to become our God making Him our Lord over everything, which is what God really wants from us as human beans.

> 18. *"But you shall remember the Lord you God: for He that gives you power to get wealth, that He may establish His covenant which He swear to your father, as it is this day." Deuteronomy 8:18 KJV*

POWER is Authority in the earth with ever VIST, to get MONEY! True wealth is asset, with revolving currency. Wealth is your money making money. You have to work to get wealth thought; you have to work even herded to maintain wealth once you have acquired wealth! God said He is the giver, so wealth has a purpose! God allows you to acquire wealth because gave His word to our far fathers, and He always keeps His word. Can you get with and it controls you, yes every good and perfect gift comes from God. God wants your obedience. Gods' Spirit will put you in the right place, at the right time, around the right people, to be blessed, to be a blessing.

Once you make Jesus your Lord, and you have

believed Gods' word by speaking it in faith to Him! God, want us to trust Him, He wants us to believe in Him no matter what it look like! Money does not fall from the sky. Money takes an intense effort to acquire it. God has make it, were if you truly trust in Him to be your source. His Spirit will lead you into the wealth He has planned for your life.

I know it is possible to walk with the Lord, He want to fellowship with you. If you have not met my Lord Jesus, He: lived, and walked on the earth, so these words can change your mind forever. If you live the life obedient to Gods' Spirit He will lead you into lasting wealth and riches. God, told our far farther Abram:

> *"Now the Lord had said to Abram, "Get you out of your country, and from your kindred, and from your father's house, to a land that I will show you: and I will make of you a great nation, and I will bless you, and make your name great: and you shall be a blessing: and I will bless them that bless you, and curse him that curses you: and in you shall all families of the earth be blessed." Genesis 12:1-3 KJV*

See being that my Heavenly Father has put Lets Get Real Ministry in my heart in December of 2006 I must give this words to you NOW, so you can walk freely in your blessed state, with the wealth your Heavenly Father Intended for you to walk with in Him. Before we move forwarded you have to be real with yourself, and by reading this your life is changing you have made the first step.

Like our ancestor you actively make God your God. Making God your God like our great, great, great grandfather Abram, God is well pleased. I know our Lord will give you a great understanding of *Genesis 12:1-3*. It is even more important to have an understanding of *Deuteronomy 8:18*. Having the knowledge and understand of true wealth that God has planned for us to have, this is my life to give to every believer that wants the God given knowledge. We all are designed to help each other, helping each other will never end in the earth. There are many misconceptions about Biblical wealth; people think that wealth and riches are not associated with holiness or godliness.

Most think that it is not right for the Child of God to be prosperous. God wants us all to be prosperous in

Walk in your NOW

health first, then in money or riches. I cannot grasp the fact that poverty is associated with godliness, when our Father made everything you see, why would any one thing God want any of us to live in poverty?

This is a myth, and a tradition I plan on uprooting this NOW, the name of our Lord and saver Jesus' name. With the authority Jesus has put in me once I have believed in Him! This myth that the poorer you are the godlier you are will stop NOW! Wealth is a tool to accomplish the mission and vision of our Heavenly Father for the earth. There are more scriptures about wealth, and money, even more about healing making all that will believe whole!

To me if you have the real reason for wealth in your heart, the better life becomes for you. Making the Lord the head of your life and then all things are possible with god! Let's look at the differences and similarities, between the words prosperity and wealth. Prosperity means: to do well, be favored, be at ease, in peace and security, totality, to be on a successful journey.

Wealth means: strength, power, goods, the ability to effect, an army, capability, and influential, upper class, to be firm, finally to accumulate enough. I hear a lot of preacher talking about prosperity preacher as if it is bad?

If they know they are talking about the very thing they should be teaching their flocks they would be ashamed of talking down on true prosperity, to me when I hear this even from the moth of a man of God they are only showing their interagency loudly!

If they know that prosperity is a journey, a walk with God, fulfilling the purpose that our Father put in their hearts as kids! To me their asking for help, if their knocking prosperity, my Lord says having Heaven on earth, as it is in Heaven! I don't know what bible their reading, how every I believe every Word that in mind, not just some parts! I think they don't know that wealth in not defined by how much money you have alone!

Strength is ability to get wealth; it's not just physical strength. It is an ability to exert to exert power to get wealth in order to fulfill my Fathers covenant. When you exert your selves, you will make an impact on the earth. When you have the resources to back up you efforts to please my Father with your talents, then you will make an even more honorable impact on earth! You tell me who pays any attention to the poor for real?

However, when you are rich in the world eyes, rich people are heard to the poor,

> 15. *"The rich man's wealth is his strong city: the destruction of the poor is their poverty." Proverbs 10:15 KJV*

There is knotting new under the sun just different ways of doing them! Me I know where my wealth comes from! Do you, do you know where your wealth comes from?

See being real with the Lord your promise things with no sorrow, and biblical wealth is a strength that comes from the Lord here on earth,

> 11. *"The rich man's wealth is his strong city, and as an high wall in his own conceit." Proverbs 18:11 KJV*

This is to me why people, even some men of God they don't know this. Think if the Kingdom of God acquires wealth for the Kingdom, the Kingdom will become a strong city in its self. As a child of God you must be very careful, you do not know what god they made promise to.

Just looking on the outside or looking at what they have, how they got it! NOW if the person can keep it then you know who gave it to them! Only God adds thing with no sorry attached to them.

Your Heavenly Father wants you His Child to have more than enough! He wants you to come out of your Egypt, the place of bondage or stronghold the world's system has operation in you.

> *"And I am sure that the king of Egypt will not let you go, no not by a mighty hand. And I will stretch out My hand, and smite Egypt with all My wonders which I will do in the midst thereof: and after that he will let you go. And I will give this people favor in the sight of the Egyptians: and it shall come to pass, that, when you go, you shall not go empty: But every woman shall borrow of her neighbor, and of her that sojourn in her house, jewels of silver, and jewels of gold, and raiment: and you shall put them upon your sons and upon your daughters; and you shall spoil the Egyptians." Exodus 3:19-22*

Know what you go thought is to perfect you, He will

Walk in your NOW

never let you leave, or pass a test empty-handed if you just let Him lead you! The year of 2008 is the year of new beginnings, for seven years you have to put up or save. Because seven years latter there will be a lack so this is the time for you to multiply and be fruitful.

"And the children of Israel were fruitful, and increased abundantly, and multiplied, and waxed exceeding mighty; and the land was filled with them. Now there arose up a new king over Egypt, which knew not Joseph. And he said to his people, behold, the people of the children of Israel are more and mightier than we: Come on, let us deal wisely with them; less they multiply, and it come to pass, that, when there, and it come to pass, that, when there falls out any war, they join also to our enemies, and fight against us, and so get them up out of the land. Therefore they did set over them taskmasters to afflict them with their burdens. And they built for Pharaoh treasure cities, Pithom and Ramses. But the more they afflicted them, the more they multiplied and grew. And they were grieved because of the children of Israel" Exodus 1:7-12 KJV

Your life will become a testimony as you prosper, because your stories will bring someone else to Christ. In the Kingdom of God system, the highest form of power is prayer, in the world's system, the highest form of power is money. When your Heavenly Father gives you riches, you want have the worlds hang ups!

Look at most of the famous people, how they are so measurable! True wealth is a gift from your Heavenly Father.

19. "Every man also to whom God has given riches and wealth, and to take his portion, and to rejoice in his labor; this is the gift of God." Ecclesiastes 5:19

2. "A man to whom God has given riches, wealth, and honor, so that he desires yet God gives him not power to eat thereof, but a stranger eats it: this is vanity, and it is an evil disease." Ecclesiastes 6:2 KJV

Walk in your NOW

The things you have possessions of are sign of the blessing, and favor of God on your life. See the car I drive was a gift from my Father. I wanted a truck, however He saw fit for me to have it and He has made a way for me to pay my bill every month by trusting in him being obedient! See if you give your tithe, He promises to hold back the devourer on your sake, my life is a living wetness on this, and God keeps His word!

Our Father wants us all to prosper, NOW when a stranger (a non-believer) to take advantage of Gods' principles (eats of, or totally believes in) in God site this is evil. God still has to keep His word. I was one of the strangers who played with the principles, and eat of the fruits! So when my Heavenly Father got tired of me playing with Him He took everything, except my big screen TV and clothing!

Me I know the system works my company prospered greatly. All my dreams of having a construction company, for 6yr 10 month span fail apart in two weeks. NOW we the Children of God, really need to align all of our thinking with the Word of God, we have the blessing.

"And it shall come to pass, if you shall

> *hearken diligently to the voice of the Lord your God, to observe and to do all His commandments which I command you this day, that the Lord your God will set you on high above all nations of the earth: And all these blessings shall come on you, and overtake you if you shall hearken to the voice of the Lord your God. Blessed shall you be in the city, and blessed shall you be in the field. Blessed shall be the fruit of your body, and the fruit of your ground, crease of your kine, and the flock of your sheep." Deuteronomy 28:1-4 KJV*

This is the Word, I know you have heard people say I'm blessed, saying that is more to it then saying it, YES, it is good to say it, but do you know what comes with it? You must know that there is a tangible and intangible evidence of wealth. There is material demonstration of the wealth of God, they are: Land, Animals, and Servants. The intangible wealth is a byproduct of tangible things; capability is the ability to do a job well, with skillfulness.

> 6. *"The land of Egypt is before you: in the best of the land make your father and*

Walk in your NOW

brethren to dwell; in the land of Goshen let them dwell: and if you know any men of activity among them, then make them rulers over my cattle." Genesis 47:6

Too much is given much is expected, you have to get as much information as you can about your skills, that you were blessed with from the Holy Spirit. The more you know about your skills the better they are for you to do the well of your Father for your life. Your Father gave you many, many, many skills it up to you to use them. So be skillful, we are people of many ability. God use your skillfulness to get wealth in your hands

11. *"and now, my daughter, fear not: I will do to thee all that thou requires: for all the city of my people doth know that thou art a virtuous woman." Ruth 3:11*

Ruth had the ability to get things done, because of her commitment to Gods' plans for her life, Joseph could get thing done as well because of his believeth in the dreams and visions God gave him.

> *"And Joseph was brought down to Egypt; and Potiphar, an officer of Pharaoh, the captain and chief executioner of the royal guard, an Egyptian, bought him from the Ishmaelite who had brought him down there. But the Lord was with Joseph, and he though a slave was a successful and prosperous man; ad he was in the house of his master saw that the Lord was with him and that the Lord made all that he did to flourish and succeed in his hand." Genesis 39:1-3 amp*

Once you believe in the plans God has for your life, then you put corresponding intense action behind what God said believing whole hearted. There is no good thing God will keep from you. It is time you really seek God in everything so the wealth God has for you can walk in it NOW.

ABOUT THE AUTHOR

I was born in Huntsville, Texas at 7:11 AM on April 29, 1978. The first time I heard the Lord's voice, I was five years old. At that time, I did not ask or know who He really was. I did not know it was the Spirit of God keeping me my whole life until writing this book. "He", the voice told me, "To not be afraid of Him". He told me He would assure me of whom He was in time. He showed me things and talked with me, as though I was the most important person in the whole world. I know you say I was only five, even more, only a child. My mom will tell you I was different from most kids.

I know now, He is my true Father; I had many men throughout my life that made an impact. I did not have a man like the voice. He was my friend; I could count on Him all the time. The voice always did what He said He would do for me. He told me all the time how much He loved me. He told me one day I would lead billions of people into the light for Him. He promised me His words were true. Everything He said about me made me feel important. It made me feel like I was needed for something bigger, by always keeping His word. That was important to me as a child even more now.

The things the voice told me all came true, so I

enjoyed talking with Him. He told me what would happen when I did what He asked of me to do. Most of the time, what He asked me to do was not only for me, it helped others too. He appeared to me in many ways.

When I was about to turn 26, He came as a man in dream that was so real. He told me His name is Jesus; He said I spent a lot of time talking with him when I was younger. He said, "I talked with him a lot until I was about twelve. He reminded me how He kept me happy. He knew how to make me feel very important when He talked to me.

As I got older, I didn't talk with him every day; however, the time we spent together when I was a child is truly priceless to me. As time passed I tried to talk to people about the things the voice told me, I talked about the things He showed me and how they all came true. I could not find any one that could understand the questions I asked about the things I saw.

Most people thought that I was crazy; some even still think the same today and try to brush me off. They could not understand or tell me why I was shown those things. I have never shared this with anyone until now. My childhood was not bad; I only remember schooling in 1st grade and then my memory skips to when I was in the 4th. The voice had showed me an aircraft that was going to be destroyed. He had shown it to me going straight up and then exploding in the atmosphere. I built this aircraft, put it in the 4th grade science fair, and won first place. One years later the space shuttle Challenger explodes on national TV in 1986, I was not shocked because the Voice told me it would happen.

He told me about so many things: spaceships, and animals, even trucks and cars that had not be thought of or found in the earth. Before I turned 12, the voice told me He would not speak to me as much. I remember Him saying, "He will keep me, and there would come a time when He would ask me what He wanted me to do for Him."

I grew up around pastors, but I didn't want to be like them! They lived two different lives; they were one way at church and another way at home. He then showed me some of His plans for my life, gave me a purpose, and I made a deal with him. I asked for seven things to happen before I was 26 years old. He said He would do them, and then I agreed with the Spirit of God that I would live for Him after this occurred.

I was allowed to know and even to see things that I sometimes could not put into words. I lived in Huntsville Texas until the second half of my freshmen year in high school. Then, I moved to Beaumont, Texas, attending and graduating from West Brook Senior High School.

I played football, ran track, and even tried to play baseball I loved to draw. I could draw anything I would see physically with my eyes, even more I enjoyed drawing the things imagine from what I was showed from the Voice.

I wanted to go to an art school just to draw, until my 10th grad year at Westbrook sir where my portfolio was stolen. I meet the architecture teacher in the hall way that day. He said, "I know who you are, you're that guy that can draw. You should come to my class and I'll show you how to draw, and make real money. As much as I loved to draw, football took me to college.

I went to Howard Payne University in Brownwood, Texas to study art and played football. NOW that I look back, the spirit of God has always kept me. He always positions me right where He wants me to be. I didn't know that HPU. Was a Christian College, it was one of the seven things I asked the voice to do. It was to play college football. Funny thing is I could have gotten a degree in ministry at HPU; however I did not want to be a pastor, or have anything to do with religion. I grew to love construction as a young man. I was around it from the age of nine; I was introduced to construction by lay grass for a man by the name of Billy Rigsby. May his soul rest in peace; I wanted to become an architect and draw blue prints because they made a lot of money drawing.

I ended up in the Art Institute of Houston for Architecture Design. I graduated with an associate's degree at the age of 19; as soon as I learned to draw blue prints on the computer, I started looking for contract. I used the projects as my school work. Once I graduated I already had projects I was working on so I started my own company ATS Design Inc. I dreamed of having a design build farm, a one stop shop. I ran ATS Design Inc., having a design build farm of my own; it was one of the seven things I asked the Voice to give me as well. ATS Design Inc. was very good to me until two weeks before my 26th birthday.

The Angel of the Lord God came and told me that it was time to be about my Father's business. It was the same man's voice I had heard when I was young. This time, He was not as friendly. He was very straight forward and about business. Even more, I had not heard him since I was 12. Too much happened within a two week period so the short version is that. He came to me twice and spoke to me. "It is time to be about your Father's business!"

I publicly announced the purpose that God has created me to do for Him on January 22, 2006. I delivered my first sermon on April 9, 2006 at Mt. Zion Baptist Church in Huntsville, Texas about "how to truly be blessed by God" where my God Father the senior Pastor at that time Melvin McCarter R.I.P. I love you Mr. McCarter. You will be greatly missed; I will never let the world miss you, and how great of a man and father you were. I will keep the faith by keeping my hand to the plow.

"Much Prayer Much Power, little prayer little power, no prayer no power" this was what he closed with every time he preached.

Throughout my life God always had some man or woman to cross my path telling me I look like a preacher. I would always say, "What does a preacher look like?" He always put men and women of God in my life at the right time in order, to strengthen my faith in Him.

I have set at tables and worked with men like Bishop I. V. Hilliard. I've met men like Bishop T. D. Jakes, and my favorite ministry Creflo Odollar. God moved me from Texas, placing me in Lawrenceville, Georgia in March of 2009. He then allowed me to meet Bishop John W. Pace and the Prophetic Campaign.

I was affirmed in the office of an Apostle by men to

become what God had said I was to Him; His special massager, a sent one of Jesus Christ. My affirmation was December 4, 2010 at Life church of Ga. That is a little about me, now let's get into why you are reading this book.

Let's Get Real Ministry

"Changing Real Peoples' Lives with the Living Word of God"

Building Houses of Refuge

We would love to connect with you. Write us, send an e-mail, we want to align with you so the body of Christ will become one, living in harmony, on one accord in: Mind, Spirit, and Body, worshiping in spirit and truth, doing the will of our Heavenly Father.

For the Kingdom of Jesus Christ to be glorified in the earth, once all of God's children are on one accord, there is nothing He will keep from us!

Our Heavenly Father will soon become well please with all of His children in the earth.

We do not believe in hierarchy, there is only one King; there is only one Lord, which is Jesus the Christ. We believe in the virgin birth of Jesus Christ as the begotten Son of God, Jesus death, barrel, to His resurrection with His assignation to now set on the right hand of our Heavenly Father interceding on our behalf!

We believe in divine alignment, with accountability,

leading into discipleship, into stewardship, being directed by the leading and guidance of the Holy Spirit. To understand the gifts and talents God has freely given to all that love Him, and would choose to live for Him, you are blessed to be a blessing. Jesus is on His way back, I pray you are ready. It is your time, it is your season remember

Walk in your Now!

Thanks for taking time out of your life and sharing it with me. I, Aundrae T. Shaw on behalf of Lets Get Real Ministry International, believe in prayer, we will always pray for Gods' will for your life by leading of the Holy Spirit; until next time God Speed.

Email: apostleashaw@gmail.com ; Aundrae Shaw; YouTube channel

www.ingramcontent.com/pod-product-compliance
Lightning Source LLC
Chambersburg PA
CBHW042022150426
43198CB00002B/37